Traveling in Time of Danger

Traveling in Time of Danger

Cathy Smith Bowers

Iris Press

First Edition

ISBN 0-916078-47-7

Library of Congress
Catalog Card Number: 98-89703

Cover Painting:
Reft II (detail) by Carol Minarick

Cover and Page Design:
Robert B. Cumming, Jr.

Iris Press
1345 Oak Ridge Turnpike
Suite 328
Oak Ridge, TN 37830

www.irisbooks.com

Acknowledgments

The author thanks the editors of the following journals:

Alkali Flats: "Kwanza," "Touring the Berliner Dom," and "In Salzburg, Austria, a Student Learns His Father is Dead"
America: "Mother Land"
The Atlantic Monthly: "The Entry" and "Learning How to Pray"
Emrys Journal: "Weather"
The Georgia Review: "You Can't Drive The Same Truck Twice," "Snow," and "Orchids"
The Greensboro Review: "Kingdom"
The New England Review: "For the Body"
Poet Lore: "Sequoia," "Pacific Time," and "Sleeping With My Brother"
Poetry: "A Southern Rhetoric"
Poetry Miscellany: "Them" and "Traveling in Time of Danger"
Shenandoah: "Easter"
Southern Review: "Sponges," "Groceries," "Slow," "Peripheral Resurrections," "From Rome," and "The Scar "
Southern Poetry Review: "Women Dancing With Babies On Their Hips" and "Bark"
Third Coast: "Flood," "The Proposal," and "Three"

For my brothers and sisters: Tricia, Gary, Rosie, Allen,

and Paul

October 26, 1958—November 26, 1997

This book is also for those people, more than I can name, who lovingly cared for and accompanied my brother as far as they could possibly go: his beautiful companion Bill Sawyer; Pedro Ayala; Stuart Sawyer; Cathy Johnson; Tabitha Romero; Sara Hummel; Dr. Suzan Stringari; Dr. Craig A. Lindquist; Aunt Juanita and Uncle Henry; Mary Helen McManus Smith, who gave us the gift of Paul; and, of course, for Jerry.

CONTENTS

Mother Land

Learning How to Pray

The secret
of this journey is to let the wind
blow its dust all over your body,
to let it go on blowing,
to step lightly, lightly
all the way through your ruins,
and not to lose
any sleep over the dead, who surely
will bury their own
don't worry.

—James Wright

Mother Land

Sponges

I bought two sponges
from a woman in Tarpon Springs.
A friend had rented a car
to drive me there
through banyan and orange grove,
the waxy frangipani,
bawdy as whores, through
the wild, throaty
lushness of hibiscus,
to the graying dock
where evening fishermen
held high for the curious
crowds their glittering catch.
And there she was, moving
from basket to basket,
enumerating for the indifferent
browsers the many possibilities
of sponge. This one for dishes.
This for marble and wood.
And, oh, these for the body,
for breast and arm and thigh,
for ankle and shin. Her face glowed
and her finger trembled
as she pointed to the delicate
layers, the thousand cells
through which once flowed
the salty current. And I saw
the deep pores of her own hands
through which she too had begun
the slow emptying. Saw with what love
she held them for our inspection
turning each toward the light,
those many vacant chambers.

Women Dancing With Babies on Their Hips

We had travelled to that old coast,
six hours to New Bern, the long ferry
from Cedar Island to Okracoke and then
to Roanoke where Manteo, for love
of the glittering English, killed Wanchese,
and so began, even from within,
that long, slow clearing.

And that night, tourists sick
of the bloody ending of our beginning,
we went for beer and music
on the deck of the Jolly Roger
where in the starry distance
lighthouses stayed the blown
shoals of islands like paperweights.

It was there we saw them, their separate
bodies swaying among the couples
coupling on the dance floor, two women,
alone, dancing with babies on their hips,
weaving in and through, stitching up
the random piece-goods of the night.

They were banners. Their hair
starfish lit. Their faces the blossomy
bright shock of sand dollars
when you find them whole.

How useless our wondering the whereabouts
of their men, imagining them away,
some war they did not belong in,
or too late back from the shrimping boat,
and tired, to join them here. These women,

their strong lovely hips dipping
and cresting, their babies' heads
flung back in a whirl of toothless
laughter, loving the lone ride,
their wild, dumb entry into the world.

Mother Land

I pitied the other children
their skinny mothers. Nothing to burrow
when the church pew began to harden
like sugar-brittle or God. Their elbows
sharp as crags we climbed to the bluff
where Jimmy Adams took our dare
and jumped and never came up again. I pitied
them their mothers, all point and longitude,
tentative as sandbars the chain gang
dozed to stay the river banks. My mama

was a continent, *terra softa*
where she sprawled in her big chair
or across the bed when thunder ripped
the shingles and rain swelled the sills
like ripe earth. And there in the valleys
of blankets and pillows, each of us staked claim
to whatever fleshy region we had chosen to settle
while the storm spent itself. My sisters
nestling the soft slopes of her breasts, me floating
meridians of hip and thigh. My mama
was promised land and we, small redoubts
not even our father could penetrate, odd denizen

from that country of men we could see
mounting the horizon, their bright
flags flying, their cannons aimed.

Snow

It was the only act of intimacy
I ever witnessed between them—that joke
my father told her, his opening
line...*I hope it snows so deep*...and then
how, for the punch, he reached out
and pulled her to him, to whisper words
that sent her red and slapping
at his khaki shirt and then her hand
lifting to his chin to remove
the little ghosts of cotton
that fluttered there. Our teachers
had sent us home from school calling
See you Monday that Thursday in December
as we ran crazed into the schoolyard
and to our separate houses
to hold vigil for that white coming,
that promise we wanted so badly to believe
we could feel, already in the graying
sky, its soft descent. All evening
the heater roared its warmth
into the room as we talked
of snow-cream so cold it hurt
your head, the fine spin a hubcap gives
down a hill of white. But by the close
of second shift, all that had shown
was a stray, barking beneath
the streetlight, our father in from the mill,
blowing the night from his hands
and telling that joke, his mouth burrowing
into the smell of our mother's hair,
and somewhere, breaking dim above the smokestacks,
a few odd stars no one would admit to seeing.

Them

Jews and niggers, my father
walking in from work
or glancing up from the daily news
would shake his head and mumble
though no verb or adjective followed or preceded
to help distinguish his blessing from his curse.

I had seen one of each. Annie
in the lunchroom where I went to school
who scraped beans and carrots
from our trays into the slop,
while Abram—strange immigrant
from some place we could not pronounce—
shoveled coal into the furnace far below.
At recess we could see him near the chutes
turned, from his labour, almost black as Annie.
We held our distance, as father had warned,
and afternoons sat full in our warm desks
keeping our perfect letters inside their lines.

One day we saw the two of them
talking in that safe space
between the garbage cans and school.
We had gathered at the window
to watch a bluejay
terrify from tree to tree an owl
that even from our small view
seemed not to belong quite there
the clumsy head, heavy hook of its body
dragging air
as if sky were a river
where someone had recently drowned.

Groceries

I had a boyfriend once, after my mother
and brothers and sisters and I
fled my father's house, who worked
at the Piggly Wiggly where he stocked
shelves on Fridays until midnight
then drove to my house to sneak me out,
take me down to the tracks by the cotton mill
where he lifted me and the quilt I'd brought
into an empty boxcar. All night
the wild thunder of looms. The roar of trains
passing on adjacent tracks, hauling
their difficult cargo, cotton bales
or rolls of muslin on their way
to the bleachery to be whitened, patterned
into stripes and checks, into still-life gardens
of wisteria and rose. And when the whistle
signalled third shift free, he would lift me
down again onto the gravel and take me home.
If my mother ever knew, she didn't say, so glad
in her new freedom, so grateful for the bags
of damaged goods stolen from the stockroom
and left on our kitchen table. Slashed
bags of rice and beans he had bandaged
with masking tape, the labelless cans,
the cereals and detergents in varying
stages of destruction. Plenty
to get us through the week, and even some plums
and cherries, tender and delicious,
still whole inside the mutilated cans
and floating in their own sweet juice.

The Proposal

Each Christmas my brother
gathers us around in the tinseled
light of our mother's house
and kneels at the feet of the newest
woman in his life and with the flair
of men in old movies
asks her to marry him. He is aging
handsome, his pale hair receding
at his temples, the lines radiating
from his eyes like tiny oriental fans
opening into the narrowing heat
of his life. Each woman is more beautiful
than the last and younger, though it is
us he turns his face to
as he proclaims the redundant litany
of his love. We smile. Applaud
his happiness so brief we can see it washing
from his face the way a restless ghost
passes through the flesh of the living.
The way years ago, after the cranberries
and turkey, the bright wrapping
curling like discarded veils amid the flames,
we could see our father's face darken
as he began to weep. All afternoon he would weep
where he sat at the periphery
of our muted play, my sisters soothing
their tongueless dolls, my brother
grinding into the floor
the wheels of his new train.

My Father's Last Wish

When they called me from the hospital
to say you had slipped into a coma
I told them, though you had requested
otherwise, to plug you back
into the machinery of this life
and I would hold you hostage
the way you held us all those years,
prisoners of your bitterness and rage.

And I would pace at your bedside, amid
the bottles and wires and tubes
the way on drunk nights you staggered
from room to room, setting each naked bulb
ablaze as your wife and children
watched, hidden, from the floorboard of the car.

And when I was good and ready, when I
had tired of rubbing the yellow
lamp of your body—forty years worth—I
would be the one to tell the doctors when.
The way, deep into those nights, it was I
who walked quietly through the rooms
of that big house, turning
all the lights you'd left burning
out.

The Bill

When I received the bill,
Father, for your death,
statement of goods
and services rendered,
I took up my calculator
and began ticking in
the dollars and cents claimed
down the funeral home's
itemized account: $225
for your embalming, $63.50
for transferral of your
remains, $34.98 for your tie
and socks and underwear.

Funny how they'd referred to me
as *buyer*, they the *seller*
as if, after a long journey alone,
I had stopped by choice
at some roadside stand
to stretch and browse and select
among the many wares—tomatoes,
cantaloupe and corn, the sweet chambered
lushness of peppers, still rich
with the good black smell of earth.

I confess I didn't want to pay
but got out the pen and checkbook
anyway, signed my name
and scrawled the total in,
knowing how sometimes
we're asked to pay up twice.
Once for what we never had.
Once for when it's taken back.

A Southern Rhetoric

"It's a sight in this world
the things in this world
there are to see," my mother says
as she hurries between the stove
and Sunday table. She is just back
from vacation. Happy.
Talking mountains. Talking rivers.
Big cedars and tidal bores.
When I tease her for redundancy,
her face glows like a sturgeon moon
risen above fat buttery atolls
of biscuits, steaming promontory
of roast. She shakes her finger
in my face and scolds me good:
"Girl, don't you forget who it was
learned you to talk."

Amazing she would want
to lay claim to these syllables
piling up like railroad salvage
when I speak, to these words slow as hooves
dredging from the wet of just-plowed fields.
I watch her turn, embarrassed, to the sink,
to the pots and pans she will scrub
to a gleam so bright we can see ourselves
as if the two of us stared back
from the lost rhetoric of memory.
From the little house, the crib
where she bent each day, naming
for me the world where words always fail,
warranting, now and then,
those few extra syllables,
some things spoken twice.

Kwanza

When I sent my uncle the Kwanza
Christmas card, black cubist Christ,
each angle of his visage full and visible

like the fractured-back-together-again
women of Picasso, when I sent my uncle
this card printed on recycled paper,

uncle I had been always a little
partial to, diagnosed by the State *simple
schizophrenic*, meaning not dangerous

to society or himself though dysfunctional
enough to qualify for the small check
they mailed to him each month for food

and warmth and shelter. *My salary*, he told
me once, *payment for staying out of the looney
bin* (he even—God knows—gets raises

like the rest of us every now and then.)
When I sent my uncle this card, he jumped
on his bike and peddled to my mother's house

where the two of them shook their heads
and in quiet deliberation decided
to call a meeting. I don't know what

happened there, not having been invited,
though my sister told me she was told
everyone showed up—Aunt Juanita and Uncle

Henry. Harold and Aunt Gladys. Loma and Dub
and Willie Mae—each bearing a pot-luck
dish to be spread on Mama's table when business

was done. It was not so much the recycled paper,
she told me she was told, or the black
Christ (some of the finest people they'd ever

known—don't get them wrong—were colored)
but those three mysterious words, *Peace
and Light*, I had scribbled between the card's

generic message and my name. Told me she
was told how each in turn hugged
my mother, wrung their hands and pondered

what he or she, in my tender years, might
have done to prevent what I had come to.
Told me she was told how in the end—after

the chicken and potatoes, the biscuits, the tea
and green bean casserole, the plates and forks
put back in their proper place—they decided

there was nothing anyone could do
so let it pass. Told me she was told
how my uncle's weathered tires

rode him safely home, my card
tucked deep inside the pocket of his coat.
How the night frogs keened

a song he'd not remembered hearing.
And something   something
not quite right

about the moon

My Mother, Ralph Kramden, and God

*One of these days, Alice. One
of these days*! Ralph Kramden's bus-driver voice
would threaten as whole families in good-hearted

American anger shook their fists into Saturday night's
black and white glow of The Honeymooners. Outside
beneath a corrugated sky of stars, bomb shelters

flickered their snowy network across the lawns
and how sweet it was, my sister and me, after Alice
and Ralph had made up once again and our mother

and father had climbed the long separate stairs
to their beds. How sweet those wild boys we knew
were waiting at the corner of Eleventh and Elm,

their souped-up Chevy humming and sputtering
as we crawled in for the climb up Cemetery Bluff.
Later, as streetlights began their timed dying-out,

they would drop us off, our backs and thighs
a throbbing grid of coils and springs. And always,
just as we turned, quiet, onto the path leading

to our porch, certain we'd pulled it off this time,
our mother's voice, tired and other-worldly, floating
from the window above—*I'll get you, just you wait,*

tomorrow, and we imagined a ghostly fist rising
out of her sleep as if we and our little crime
existed only in the bad neighborhood of her dreams.

But by tomorrow she had somehow forgotten her threat
that seemed to drift like fallout onto our heads,
like soot from the millyard smokestack

that dirtied the laundry she had so carefully
hung. And we, like Alice, had again escaped
the Great One's wrath. That house is gone now.

Those boys. My sister cities away
and Jackie Gleason dead. Bomb shelters obsolete
as the backseats of cars, now that we die for love.

Still, who could help but wonder exactly what it was
my sister and I and Alice had night after night
escaped. Or if we had escaped at all, knowing

how the channels sometimes cross and the voices
blur—*I'll get you, just you wait, tomorrow.*
How in the truant heart that old fist still shakes.

BRINGING BACK THE DEAD

There is this little game
        my niece wants to play
                when she visits, that I played

when I was a child, that I
        taught her to play. She offers
                me her hand she has made into a fist

and I wrap my own around her wrist,
        delicate-veined, blue with the young oxygen
                of her blood, and squeeze it tight,

cutting off the circulation, though
        not enough to hurt, and with my other hand
                begin to knead and rub the knot

of palm and knuckles, dirty
        from the labor of her play. I rub
                the magic lamp of her small fist

and signal her to open, then count
        each bloodless finger one by one. Again
                she closes. I knead and rub. She opens

and I count. We repeat
        until her fingers wither, pale
                as asparagus spears the Chinese

harvest for their tenderness in the dark.
        Why is it we keep returning to this game
                she calls *bringing back the dead?*

Knowing how we fear them, trusting
        the heavy angels, the stone toes pressing.
                Stay put! they seem to warn, spreading

their wings above the fresh-turned earth.
     And always shrieks of dread
          and laughter fill the room

when at the final moment of our game,
     she opens and I count again, then reach
          into the center of her shriveled palm,

drawing my fingers upward
     as I release the grip on her wrist
          my other hand has held.

Ghost! Ghost! She squeals,
     as the blood rushes back
          and she imagines some lost spirit

swimming her body into the world again.
     I laugh and explain the principles of blood,
          physiology of artery and vein

as one day she will explain
     to her daughter, after loosening
          the grip on her wrist

and something neither of them can see
     goes rafting. And she, too, will insist
          on the likelihood of spirits,

as I, great aunt, dead
     and long forgotten, rise,
          through the wash of her tiny palm,

ignoring the blood's easy logic,
     the granite weight of angels.

STRING

"You've got a string hanging,"
my sister says, and we all
look down at my tattered leggings,
the ones I pull on—dirty or
clean—when I need something old,
some ancient softness
against the worn and calloused
sorrows of the flesh. We look down,

I, my sister, niece, and brother-in-law,
to the gray thread dangling from the hole
three quarters of the journey up my inner thigh,
in dangerous proximity to that
place—that dark crossroads
still unnameable here in the rural
South. My brother-in-law reaches

deep into the pocket of his pants
and pulls out his lighter, pretending
to ignite it like a fuse or wick.
I jump back and scream as he breaks
wild and uncontrollable into laughter,
unstoppable guttural roar of this man
who two days and two nights has not
for his just-dead father stopped crying.

Who gives in, now, to this moment,
to the odd and sudden grace of silliness,
the unpronounceable god of string.

Weather

Even the ancient Egyptians
knew God was nothing
more than weather,
a warm, dry wind
surfing the Nile's easy swell
as Osiris drove his faithful chariot
across the sky. It's why
they tried to take it with them,
lugging into their tombs
their worldly possessions—pots
and pans, tables and chairs,
and the favored servants,
gone out on the pharoah's finest stuff.
Meanwhile, next door, the bug-eyed Sumerians
quaked between the wild, impossible surge
of the Tigris and Euphrates, dreading
the grave, fearing they might awaken
into another life of flood and storm.

It's no wonder barbers live
the longest and happiest lives.
All day that old confession of weather
passing from chair to chair
and the hum of shears
climbing the ridged and snowy slopes
of all those necks.

It's no wonder the last love
of my grandmother's life
was the weatherman on the local channel
she kept her TV tuned to, her hair
a knot of blue against her neck

as she rocked on the porch
between updates, calling out
the latest forecast to passersby.
And no wonder each would stop a moment
out of their busy lives
to listen, to smile and nod
before moving on, taking with them
that small gift of weather, that prayer.

Learning How to Pray

Easter

"Orrys," Allen says and laughs
when he drips gravy from Mama's
porcelain dish onto the table.
It is Easter and we are speaking,
as we do at all our family gatherings,
the old language of childhood, the way
my niece began rolling the world
into words, dropping the initial "s"
and grafting it to the end
like an awkward branch from
some other family's tree.

So "sorry" is what he meant.
"Sorry" for the stain blossoming
brown as the tips of dogwood
on the lace cloth used only
for holidays. All day this language
more obtuse than the Rosetta Stone
as my niece cringes in her seat,
too old now, she believes, for such silliness.
She is just thirteen and waiting
for the blood to begin. "Anitarys,"
my sister whispers, speaking of the small napkin
she has begun to carry in her purse
and we laugh.

Later, because he is so far
away, we will phone our youngest brother
and how's "Ausalitos" our mother will ask
before passing the phone to each of us
who will speak to him of weather,
the profusion of daffodils lighting

the far pasture of the farm, though
no one will mention the disease
he carries inside him, a language
we can't yet speak, and no stone,
no stone to help us understand.

Kingdom

When my brother
finally spoke its name,
the white cells of his body
having relinquished
their ancient
instruments of war
the small bombs
silenced
and the hand grenades
the tanks slow
retreat into mirage
the horses
dismounted
and the bright swords
sheathed
the sticks
the stones
laid
finally down
and the little lost
animal of the spirit
rising
stepping its soft
hooves into the light,
I wanted
to know that peace
walk into that quiet
kingdom
to lie down
in a life like that.

SEQUOIA

Later, arm-in-arm,
we walked through
Muir Woods, its deep
and leafy symmetry older
than history, wandered
among ferns and azaleas,
through the crags of Cathedral
Grove where he stepped
suddenly into the hollow
of a giant Sequoia
and asked me to take
his picture. His breathing
was measured and heavy
as I waited for the light
to signal the camera
ready. He smiled I clicked
and again he stepped
into the world
asking if I wanted to know
how it felt when the doctors
told him he had no T-cells
left. I nodded, keeping my eyes
averted, worrying the camera
back into its worn-out
case. Free, he said, I could
breathe again. After ten years
I could breathe. Get on
with my life.

L'Art Brut

On the fifth day of my visit,
after the sweet and heady
cruise through Napa and Sonoma,
the walk along the Castro
where the homeless sick
waited for the doors

of the Cannabis Club to open—all
legal my brother assured
me—after the starry, perforated
Big Top of the Russian River,
he asks if today I could explore
alone, shop or something,

so he might rest while his weekly
artificial fix of immunity
takes hold. So I leave
to buy scarves and end-of-season
dresses, to forage the gleaming
stalls of mackerel and sole,

and in the cooling evening return,
surprised to find him kneeling
in his back yard, making, of all things,
candles. His terrace is pocked with holes
across which the rays of yellow pencils
dangle from their centers makeshift wicks.

All day he has been pouring wax, reds
and blues and greens, the salvaged
stuff of wings now hardening in each sandy

grave. I sit on the steps and watch
as he digs the earth from around each candle,
exhuming his finished products, and I see

how, before pouring the wax, he had pressed
into the sides of each hole bright shards
of colored glass, variegated stones bejeweling
the clumsy creations I help carry inside and place
along the dimming window sill. Once in Lausanne,
after the obligatory tours of Europe's finest

museums, the apples of Cezanne, Monet's lilies,
the measured elegance of the Renaissance,
I happened upon a museum filled with works
of the terminally ill, tramps, and unschooled
visionaries. *L'art brut,* I was told, then left
to wander the shuttered rooms, touching

the impossible colors, the tortured
metamorphoses of debris and olive branch,
shell effigies, the heart's self-portraits gouged
from the rotted bark of stumps. And the cell
of a man who before he died carved every square
inch—the elaborate iconography of cathedrals

coaxed from the headboard of his
bed, the floor, the walls, the sill of his
barred door. First with his
fork. And when they took away his
fork, his spoon. And when they took away his
spoon, the handle of his

chamber pot.

ORCHIDS

No wonder my brother
in that year of his life
began peopling his cliffside home
with their strong and delicate
tenacity   began foraging
the genealogy of their loveliness
as if they were kin

ancient aphrodisiacs
aristocrats of sepal and stem
star-children of the orient   it is
this story he loves best
forgets twice he has told it
and tells again   how once

in old New Guinea   a Belgian
expedition and their native guide
startled upon a show of sweet Dendrobium
sprung from a mound of skulls
ribbony wreaths marking
the forgotten unhinged door
of fontanelle   each bloom
half bird   half spider
not quite furred breast
and breath of bumblebee

on the last morning of my visit
he called me to the mirror
by his front door   said *look*
as he lifted his shirt and stared
at his own reflection   I touched
the flesh around each lesion
as if to validate the freshly

tilled soil of his body
then looked up
past him   past me
to the mirrored space
behind us   to his quiet
anthem of orchids
whose seeds store no food
who can   if they must
survive on air

Pacific Time

It is not my brother's dying
that I fear, that perfect healing
bringing him forever home,
but those three hours that will have passed
between the Pacific Time of his leaving
and the Eastern Standard news
of that good death.

Four o'clock in Sausalito
is seven here, I might have baked
a loaf of bread, the measuring
and the sifting, the kneading with my hands
the way each evening on my last visit
I would massage his back, avoiding the welts
and lesions that wouldn't heal.

I know there is some logic
to longitude's sleight of hand.
Like the televised magician
who before my eyes
made the Statue of Liberty
disappear. Later, in an interview,
he explained how he had done it
with smoke and light and mirrors.

I chose to believe it
anyway. The sky growing
dark around it. How it shimmered
for a moment and was gone.

Learning How to Pray

When I heard my brother
was dying   youngest
of the six of us   our
lovely boy   I who in matters
of the spirit
had been always suspect
who even as a child
snubbed Mama's mealtime ritual
began finally to
pray   and fearing
I would offend
or miss completely
the rightful target of my pleas
went knocking everywhere
the Buddha's huge
and starry churning   Shiva
Vishnu   Isis   the worn
and ragged god of Ishmael
I bowed to the Druid reverence
of trees   to water   fire
and wind   prayed to weather
to carbon   that sole link
to all things
this and other worldly
our carbon who art in heaven
prayed to rake and plow
the sweet acid stench of dung
to fly   to the fly's soiled
wing   and to the soil

I could not stop
myself   I like a nymphomaniac
the dark promiscuity
of my spirit   there
for the taking   whore
of my breaking heart   willing
to lie down   with anything.

SLEEPING WITH MY BROTHER

Like dreaming
and knowing while you dream
you dream
this one night—despite
propriety's ragged
manifesto—this one night
with your brother
in this one bed

all night
your front to his back
breasts to shoulder blades
belly pressed
to the long sweet
slide of spine
to the right-now-still-alive
miracle
of blood and bone

all night
you don't sleep
all night
beyond the lift
and fall of your arm
curved around the curve
of this one chest
you watch the lights
of the Christmas tree
their soft pulsing
like the chronic idling
beneath your palm

all night
like the back rider
of a down-hill run-away
sled you do the only
thing   you can do
close your eyes
and hold on

Peripheral Resurrections

Three

"It was one of those moments
you wish you could
marry forever."

—James Seay

My father, as he pulled
off his beaten shoes and unbuttoned his shirt
after a hard day in the spinning
room, the whistle he would ease through the slit
between his tongue and palate, too tired
to press his lips into the tight **o**
of the realer whistle whistled Sunday mornings
before the world went bad, the clear,
pure strains of *Fraulein* called up
from his healing lungs

Beth's snowflakes,
before she died, how, when she opened
the door to let us in, hundreds
of them she had cut and hung from the ceiling—
sloppy paper flakes spinning above the heat
of the big-bellied stove, unbelievable
soft blizzard of white

the look on Flint's face,
its sweet incredulity of loss
as if in the telling of the story
he suddenly realized the girl
in the men's restroom of that New Orleans
oyster house was the one true love of his life,
the way he turned from the urinal

and there she was, pushing him aside
pleading—*I'm going to throw up
and I'll need you to hold my hair*—
and, done, she was gone, as he stood there
stunned, still holding his penis,
his other hand cupped tight to his mouth and nose,
breathing in, breathing deep
the still lingering jasmine of her hair.

You Can't Drive the Same Truck Twice

for my ex-husband

When I heard the sudden
thunder of my husband's truck
explode into the drive
and saw him, after ramming
the defective gear-stick
into neutral, emerge crazy-eyed
and fevered, fling up
the battered hood, go down
and disappear beneath its open wound
of primer, I knew how the evening
would go. How deep into moonlight
he would hang like Jonah, half in,
half out, his full weight given
to the wrench, gripped to the stripped
bolts and nuts, capping and uncapping
the ancient battery, his body
lost to that odd carcass of scavenged parts.
I loved him for his love of broken things—
the handleless hoes and axes, the sprung
rumble seat bought years ago
at auction, the legless chairs
retrieved from garbage heaps,
that truck each day he reinvented.
Like the rivers of Heraclitus. Like Van Gogh's
olive trees and irises that quiver,
still. Bristle. As if caught forever
in the antique instant of their opening.
It's why we love Jesus, some philosopher
once said, instead of God. Why lovers
love the moon that's always falling.

The Scar

The first time I saw his naked
body rising above me
from the couch where all day
I had memorized for my art history final
the rudiments of line and medium and hue
I thought Michaelangelo's *David*
had stepped out of its binding,
the papery thighs and forearms
bulging to life, the shoulders,
the heavy penis ripped
from the glossy pages, the stone,
for centuries cupped and ready
in the perfected tension
of his hand, laid finally down.

We were eighteen then, and I had never seen
anything so beautiful—that body,
lifting from my own inadequate body,
the small breasts, the pale, skinny
arms and thighs that didn't deserve
his loveliness—and would have turned,
afterwards, self-consciously away
had it not been for the scar (emergency
appendectomy, I later learned). Had it not been
for the ragged stigmata of that wound,
purple phalanx of cells that must have rallied hard
for a boy of twelve, little army of flesh
gathering together for his life.

Years later after love, I would watch
him sleeping, his chest rippling
like a quilt laid to air against the windy grass,

his hair curled, graying, at his temples,
and I knew, finally, the wisdom
of old philosophers, how what is real
exists only in the realm of the unchanging.
Like that scar, lifting and falling,
that lovely, immutable banner of his breathing.

Wanted

Nights I crawled in beside him,
tired from his books, exhaustion
and poverty spooned between us

like the ménage-à-trois we once saw
in some dirty movie, and fell
into the long double-shift

of dreams, that conveyor belt, stinking
and gummy from the scantily wrapped
breasts of chicken and the mutilated

cans of soup and spaghettios, the nightly
joke of the meat department boys
or the ones who worked in stock, who

grabbed naps on giant sacks of Alpo
when business was slow. My ankles
throbbed in my sleep and the faces

of customers kept rising
out of the clang and roar
of registers. The long-married

couple who bought two supplies
of groceries, the bottom of their cart
like the Continental Divide

or those invisible boundaries
children swipe across the hot
backseats of cars. They would turn

their backs to each other, wadding
the damp, thin dollars to their hearts,
making sure the other couldn't see

into the stingy caverns of their separate
wallets. And the two who bought
their groceries one item at a time,

their snowy heads appearing at my counter
ten times a day for those game cards
you could scratch and match

for prizes. They never said a word
but collected their Cornflakes
or Twinkies before pausing at the sliding

doors to scrape the silvery lining
from the card as I seethed
and shoved the next customer's apples

into the innocent hands of the bagboy
at my back. It is this I will miss
years later, after the degrees, the bills

paid off and nothing left to hold us,
finally, together. This dream
I could always count on. And Sundays,

the two of us ghosting the local
post office, memorizing the faces
of murderers and thieves. Dreaming

of the rewards they carried, their scars
and stubbled faces, the beautiful broken
noses of all those saviors.

BARK

There is evidence, scientists
say, that before dogs
were domesticated, before
we rescued them from wilderness,

they howled, growled, yelped,
and whined, but did not bark.
Evidence, they say,
that hearing human

speech—*beg sit stay*—they
tried to mimic it
and got the bark instead.
Lost darling, casualty of my divorce,

surest way my husband knew
to punish me (so loved I named
you Seamus, Mr. Heaney to strangers
and acquaintances,) remember

the night I fetched you
from your pen, the hurricane
already moving inward from the coast,
how you mistook my cautionary

measure for some midnight jamboree,
soiree du chien in celebration
of something you couldn't quite remember
but must have done right that day.

That night you were too happy
to bark, pranced in jubilation
of your middle-of-the-night reprieve
around and around the couch

where at either end my husband
and I dozed in the ostensible safety
of our living room. We had learned
already the democracy of those storms.

Three years before, our yard
untouched, every oak and hemlock
pointing as ever upward, as we stared
at our neighbor's property

reduced to sticks and stones.
Not knowing what other storms
were gathering, you continued
your solitary parade around

the room, where at intervals
we would feel against our drowsy lips
that unschooled kiss, the sudden unabashed
joy of your wet tongue. Years later,

over drinks or in the grocery
check-out line, friends catching up
on the progress of our families, how suddenly
embarrassed and put off they become

when I pull out pictures of you
and the wag-tail ghost of your name
lopes across my tongue. Then the sob,
the yelp, the whine. Almost a bark.

Peripheral Resurrections

It had been the kind of day
they sing about in country/westerns:
how the drunk, the day
his mother got out of prison
to attend the funeral of his wife,
put a pistol to his head and missed,
and I just couldn't muster much enthusiasm
when I found, that evening in my mailbox,
a letter from Jacques Cousteau
insisting I alone could save the dolphin.

But later, when you stopped by
in the truck you borrowed from a friend
after your wife had wiped you out of everything,
I couldn't help but laugh at your perfected misery,
at the way your ragged face gave in
to that late-night plate of grits and sausage.

I sat, suddenly happy, watching you, brother,
and thinking of Jacques Cousteau,
his endangered angel who will dive into the depths
and with her gentle head buffet to the surface
for that first vital breath
whatever she mistakes for her just-born—
rotted oars, broken keels and rudders,
a drowning man—
though the grateful saved never knew her
and what was saved in the end
was not what she'd meant to save at all.

ASCENSION

After the hardware salesman,
I fell in love with a man who wanted
to ascend. All moondrift and solar, washed

shore and the nimbused bones of fish, his hands
a God-knead, tendering my body's own brilliant
language of grief. *Getting my light body,*

he explained, when I spoke of his thinning
arms and legs, his frame an anorexic girl's
on top of mine, the slight waist, sinewy chest

paled to the vegetable hues
of iceberg and romaine, his face
and shoulders draped in the tofu-shroud

of his flesh. But I needed evidence
of that rumored other life, so took him in.
Grunewald's most famous Christ

stepped down from his altar
into the world again. Jesus on the
lam and me, failed atheist,

ready to be washed in the blood of
anything. I learned, finally,
what it was like all those years,

my husband under the house alone,
knocking at pipes, securing the joists
and studs, the mundanities

of this life—out of my lover's
holy precinct—relegated now to me.
Battles with the shell-shocked

landlord as the floor began to sink
and the roof continued its slow leak
through the ceiling above our bed.

One night I awoke to find him
in the flung doors of the balcony.
He had taken the gauze curtains

from their rods and draped them across
his shoulders, his arms spread against
the moon's soft rising like the wings

of some angel or bat. Next morning
he was gone, transmorphosed to that place
of peace and light he'd feared my own bereft

and unenlightened soul would never know.
Ascended, I assumed, until leaving
for work I saw beyond the back door's

freshly-painted white—now splattered
in red—the four muddy ruts of his retreads
and knew he had taken the truck instead.

Flood

Lugging my second load
of dirty laundry up the long hill
between my cabin and the house,

I saw approaching in the distance
a machine so sleek and gleaming
it seemed itself a prayer

against the chronic dust
and labor of my sister's farm.
In the yard I stopped to catch

my breath, hoist the burgeoning
load of muddy socks and overalls
higher on my hip as the wheels

ground to a halt and you emerged
from the driver's side, waving
your bible above the balding Ararat

of your head. You must have been
a seasoned pilgrim in this land
of the terminally lost, for you lit

right in, afraid, perhaps, I might
turn irredeemably away before you'd had
the chance to reach the daily quota

of your witness. I stood with my mouth
agape in the unstoppable testimony
of your love, your

hi hello how are you
I'm Wendell and this is my wife Lorraine
and we'll only be a minute I promise
everyone being so busy these days
and isn't it a pity all the changes
looming before us sooner than we think
the warnings aplenty we've been sent
the snakes for instance and the flood
you've heard of Noah right? You do believe
in the flood don't you   surely you do....

Shut up, Wendell. Shut up,
I would have said had you let up
a moment. Would have said, yes,

yes, I do believe, for floods,
like certain other things, happen.
Was happening at that very moment

in my sister's laundry room, a blown
hose in the rinse cycle of my first
load and the water even as you

spoke, ascending the newly-papered
walls of her dining room and den.
When my faith has gone to flotsam.

When the closest I've lately come
to salvation is the man who followed
me one night home, who looked so much

like Jesus riding the wild surge
of my lonely thighs I let him stay a year,
I think of you, Wendell, your spate

of prophecy truer than you would ever
know, your wife keeping her safe distance
at your back, the terror in her eyes

that of a dove having been for days
aloft and still no land in sight.
And me treading the waters

of my disbelief, shifting my soiled
burden from hip to hip as at that very
moment through the faulty plumbing

of my sister's ancient Kenmore
God, as always, was moving
in his one and mysterious way.

Fat Man in the Sauna

How strange the aloneness
of that day. The deserted hotel gym
where I walked a mile in my own
shoes on a machine that numbered
the openings and closings
of my heart. Then laps in the pool,
a weightless floating of the body's
ten-thousand griefs. I had driven
for hours, after the final papers
of my divorce, and checked in
to the Renaissance Hotel, alone.
It was Christmas, everything
ashimmer in that newest Jerusalem
where anything, I hoped, might be
forgiven or healed. And there he was,
of all places, when I finished
my workout, the fattest man
I had ever seen, beardless and bald,
his white groin swaddled, half sitting,
half reclining in the cedary-sweet
warmth of the sauna, slowly eating
an apple. *Come in* he said, calmly,
quiet between bites, between
the skin's delicate breaking
and the soft ruminations
of his tongue.   *Come in* he said.

And I went in

Traveling in Time of Danger

TOURING THE BERLINER DOM, JANUARY, 1990

What I remember most
about the long descent
into the crypt
of the bombed cathedral
was not the tenured dust,
nor the scattered bones
of emperors, bones of their sons
and daughters, nor all the cherubs
tumbled, their terrible lips
and noses hacked away.
Nor how, as our guide explained,
they dug later in, experts
kicking light into the dark
like frenzied angels,
gone down to verify
which armbone, shin,
matched the startled
clavicles and ribs.
But how, after we climbed, blinded,
back into our lives, yes,
what I remember most
was how we turned
when at the perimeter of our group
a man, aged seventy, knelt
at his old wife's feet,
slowly on one knee
and tied her shoe, looped
one string carefully
across the other
and pulled it through, tightening
the worn laces into a solid bow.
We stood there quiet and watched him
tie her shoe, pat it, then turn gently
to the still-tied other one and tighten it, too.

Hair

Always, when one travels with students
there is the problem of hair,
more urgent than the Croats and Serbs,
than the repatriated Haitian
screaming *I'd rather be dead*
as he slipped the saving rope they'd tossed him
around his throat, then, flailing the waves
like the Neanderthal breast of God,
went madly under.

Again and again you explain
in your most serious teacher-voice
the practicality of converters, rudiments
of volt and charge, but they know
all voltage is the same, nudge each other
and wink, the way relatives
talk their secret talk
in the bedrooms of the dying.

So, later in the privacy of their rooms
they plug into this foreign world
that to their surprise sputters
and fizzles then glows a brighter
bright before the lights shut down,
before the entire floor
goes black as East Berlin
and the little concierge
comes stamping, pounding
the derelict air above his balding head.

You smile, reader. You smile, knowing
as well as I the importance of being coiffed,
of hair washed and blown just so
for that long journey up the Zugspitz
or, say, the drive to Dachau
where we all want to look our best
in case we see ourselves reflected
in the ovens' dull glaze, still heavy
with the memory of flesh the villagers
swore they never smelled. Or if they did,
thought it only their daughters
dressing for their handsome evening soldiers,
too dreamy to realize
they'd held the glowing rod
too long inside those delicate
human curls.

The Entry

In Paris there is a hospital
and a police station, I read
from the yellow pages of my journal,
though I had forgotten, or pushed
somehow from memory, that one pathetic entry
scrawled on our seventh day
in the most beautiful city in the world.
But there they are, years later,
those words streaked like snuff
across the page, a stagnant pond
through which her face now rises,
that bright senior dreaming of graduation,
her future almost close enough to kiss.
And there, too, the face she later recalled,
as she wept, tugging at the inadequate gown
the nurse insisted she put on. Face
of that young man who spoke no English
in his pointed snakeskin shoes
and leather jacket, dark eyes
and bushy brows that spun her pulsing
amid the colored lights of the discoteque
and then, the white interior of his car,
that room he dragged her screaming to,
strewn with women's lingerie and shoes.
And afterwards, the odd distant keen
of sirens, all night, as she lay there
still beside him, staring into the dark,
into the rest of her only life.

Traveling in Time of Danger

Outside the Gellert Hotel
the sun comes up as usual
above the Danube that keeps on going
between the sprawled, lovely banks
of Buda and Pest, despite
the pre-dawn news the airwave static
delivered to our rooms: Iraq
bombed, and little Kuwait,
as promised, now avenged.
Our families want us home.
One student begins her frantic packing
though I keep assuring her,
ironic as it may seem, that the safest
time to travel is in time of danger.
And truly, after a highjacking
or the invasion of some small place
too insignificant to note, airports
and railways burgeon with guards,
so many it seems there's one for each of us,
our own personal saviors, machine guns
slung across their breasts
like children being carried to safety.
But by now she's finished—her baggage
stuffed with tiny dolls
stiff in the obsolete clothing
of their histories—and has called a cab
to take her to the airport where she'll wait,
counting her breaths, trusting the troops
already gathering, flooding
the gates and runways. Like the rivers
of that country she'll go home to,
the rivers that must have run there
in the first days of its life,
the first good days of its life.

In Salzburg, Austria, a Student Learns His Father Is Dead

"But they were estranged,"
the students keep explaining
when I express surprise
at his decision not to go back home.
He snaps too quickly back
into the easy banter of co-eds,
laughs too loud and often
for a boy who's lost his father,
as I lost mine, twice
in this same life.
Today he'll go together
with us down
into the mines they named
the city for. Four hundred feet
below the white world
where we'll board the little ferry,
our guide a leder-hosened
Charon, laughing hard
at our bad German, at all
our exclamations
of terror and delight.
And salt! Salt crusted
everywhere! We'll touch
the hazel rock gleaming
above our heads, bring
our fingers to our tongues,
tasting the briny core, deeper
than we dreamed
we would ever have to go.

FOR THE BODY

St. Patty's Day and hordes
of would-be Irish filled the streets,
decked in their greens and high on Guinness

and blarney and everyone in love and me, too,
though I had sunk for just a moment to the curb,
dizzy from the strains of *Danny Boy*

some tattooed drunk kept wailing
in my ear. So there I was, eye-level
with that torrent of knees poking from holey

jeans, the worn and dusty boots of bikers
who'd thundered for the morning into town,
goose-bumpy thighs of teeny-boppers

rushing the season in their mini-skirts
and shorts. And I was thinking,
as I'm prone to do when I'm drunk and feeling

philosophic, about Descartes, night
after night in his little study
burning all those candles, as if

it really mattered which, the body
or the mind, is easier to know. It was then
I saw her, that skeleton of a girl, or saw,

at least, the part of her that propelled
her through the crowd, those sticks of legs,
like something dead amidst the burgeoning

mass of shins and ankles. I started to reach
for her, as if without my help she would crumple,
small mound of twig and straw before my eyes.

How she must have hated that trapping
of flesh, that albatross, jail-cell
of the spirit she would gladly be rid of.

And, yet, there it was, all over her arms
and face, that delicate growth of hair,
that halo of warmth her body in desperation

had spun, like the blown silk of milkweed,
like the bleached coat of some animal
grown long ago extinct, pale fur

the flesh in unrequited love had wrapped
her in. Then she was gone, borne
by that wave of strangers, and I, sobering,

went back to my green beer, to Descartes,
brooding above his silvery river of wax,
the exhausted wick going finally down, and out.

From Rome

Evenings I go down to the Spanish Steps
beneath the window where Keats died,
take my place among the derelicts
and lovers, and write to my family

in the mill town where I grew up. I shuffle
through postcards—Bernini's and Donatello's,
various sun-lit angles of the Coliseum,
home to the homeless cats treading

the ancient stone, the atavistic
taste of Christian still lingering
on their tongues, to the one I bought
for my uncle, the one I'm sure he's seen

in picture books, God touching
Adam to life amid the pagan sybils
and ignudi of the Sistine Ceiling.
I love knowing how he will brighten

to find something in his mail,
odd word from the world
he slipped long ago out of, though
each Thursday he appears

at my mother's door, bearing
his gift of love—two wild cherry
cough drops glistening like jewels
in the extended craziness of his hand.

He touches the tip of his old cap
and he's off again, shadowboxing
his way back home and up the long stairs
to his third floor room where he will

tape to his window this card,
its bright colors facing into the street,
as if the strangers who pass each day below
could see, if they glanced up, this Dionysian

Adam, propped on his elbow, lifting
in non-chalance his powerful finger.
And God, his hair and beard
blowing furiously in the painted wind,

the curious horde at his back, and Eve
wedged in the circle of his arm, her frail
lovely shoulders pulling away,
not much wanting that world

she alone can see waiting there
in the small hard space
between their fingertips.

Slow

I like the joke about the snail
who mugged the turtle
who when asked by the policeman
to recount the sequence of events
couldn't *because it all happened so fast.*

It's the only joke I know,
the one I always preface—*Stop me
if you've heard it*—though friends
who love me crack up each time, slap
each other on the back,
and laugh themselves to tears.

I want a life that slow.
Like George, the idiot savant,
who couldn't spell his name
or count to ten, but could remember
for the talk-show host, the weather
of any day she named—her high school
graduation, Pearl Harbor,
the day the Rosenbergs were killed.

I'll tell you the truth, he would begin,
the year washing slowly back, cresting,
sweet wave against his tongue,
the little ark of months and days
come to rest on Ararat. *June 7, 1959.*
Warm and sunny that one was, and then,
the wreck of his old hand rising toward the sky,
The truth I've told will get me into heaven.

I want a life that slow. To lumber
each morning out of the slush
and mire, my earthly possessions
strapped across my spine. And like
George, famous for making small-talk,
I'll turn to you, good friend, idling
on the stump next door, the wound-down
clock of your body glistening in the light,

and *Stop me if you've heard this*, I'll begin,
as your eyes bank with tears, happy
with this old joke, this weather,
this truth I've told, again.

Cathy Smith Bowers

• • • • • • • • • •

Cathy Smith Bowers is a native of South Carolina. She was a winner of the 1990 General Electric Award for Younger Writers and a South Carolina Poetry Fellowship. Her poems have appeared widely in publications such as *The Atlantic Monthly, The Georgia Review, Poetry, Shenandoah, The Southern Poetry Review, The Southern Review, Kenyon Review*, and many others.

Cathy's first book, *The Love That Ended Yesterday in Texas*, was published in 1992 as the first winner of the Texas Tech University Press First-book Competition in their Poetry Award Series, subsequently named for Walt McDonald. **Iris Press** republished *The Love That Ended Yesterday in Texas* in 1997.

Cathy is Poet-in-Residence at Queens College in Charlotte, North Carolina. During her years at Queens College she has also taught in the International Study Program, in which she has traveled to England, France, Italy, Hungary, Czechoslovakia, Austria, Korea, Indonesia, Malaysia, Singapore, Switzerland, Germany, and elsewhere. The organizing element of this book derives from journeys both geographical and emotional.

ABOUT THIS BOOK

This book was composed in Adobe Caslon. William Caslon released his first type faces in 1722. Caslon's types were based on seventeenth-century Dutch old style designs, which were then used extensively in England. Because of their incredible practicality Caslon's designs met with instant success. For example, printer Benjamin Franklin hardly used any other typeface, and the first printings of the *American Declaration of Independence* and the *Constitution* were set in Caslon.

♾ The paper used in this publication meets the minimum requirements of the American National Standard for Information Sciences—Permanence of Paper for Printed Library Materials, ANSI Z39.48-1984.

Printed in the United States of America
by Thomson-Shore, Inc.